Calisthenics

2nd Edition

100 Bodyweight Exercises

See Results Faster Than Ever with the Definitive Guide to Bodyweight Training

Mario Lavezzi

© **Copyright 2016 by Mario Lavezzi - All rights reserved.**

This document is geared towards providing exact and reliable information in regards to the topic and issue covered. The publication is sold with the idea that the publisher is not required to render accounting, officially permitted, or otherwise, qualified services. If advice is necessary, legal or professional, a practiced individual in the profession should be ordered.

- From a Declaration of Principles which was accepted and approved equally by a Committee of the American Bar Association and a Committee of Publishers and Associations.

In no way is it legal to reproduce, duplicate, or transmit any part of this document in either electronic means or in printed format. Recording of this publication is strictly prohibited and any storage of this document is not allowed unless with written permission from the publisher. All rights reserved.

The information provided herein is stated to be truthful and consistent, in that any liability, in terms of inattention or otherwise, by any usage or abuse of any policies, processes, or directions contained within is the solitary and utter responsibility of the recipient reader. Under no circumstances will any legal responsibility or blame be held against the publisher for any reparation, damages, or monetary loss due to the information herein, either directly or indirectly.

Respective authors own all copyrights not held by the publisher.

The information herein is offered for informational purposes solely, and is universal as so. The presentation of the information is without contract or any type of guarantee assurance.

The trademarks that are used are without any consent, and the publication of the trademark is without permission or backing by the trademark owner. All trademarks and brands within this book are for clarifying purposes only and are the owned by the owners themselves, not affiliated with this document.

Table of Contents

Introduction vii
Chapter 1: Push Ups, Pull Ups and Squats 1
    Basic Push-Up 2
    Decline Push Up 3
    Incline Push Up 4
    Clapping Push Up 5
    Crossover Push Up 6
    Knee Push Ups 7
    Diamond Push Up 8
    Handstand Push Up 9
    Spider Push Up 10
    Dolphin Push Up 11
    Single Leg Push Up 12
    Push Up with Reach 13
    Staggered Push Ups 14
    Superman Pushup 15
    Pull Ups 16
    Sternum Pull Up 17
    Inclined Pull Up 18
    Side to Side Pull Up 19
    Muscle Up 20
    Shoulder Width Chin Up 21
    Towel Grip Pull Up 22
    One Arm Chin Up 23
    The Human Flag 24
    Squats 25
    Wall Squats 26
    Pistol Squats 27

Pile Squats	28
One Legged Squat	29
Eagle Squats	30
Sumo Squat	31
Figure Four Squat	32
Squat Jacks	33
Chapter 2: Dips, Raises and Lunges	**35**
Dips	36
Chest Dips on a Straight Bar	37
Bench Dips	38
Dip to Leg Raisers	39
Incline Dip	40
One Arm Triceps Dips	41
Wall Sit	42
Leg Raises	43
Lying Leg Raises	44
Lying Torso Raises	45
Lying Side Leg Raises	46
Side Leg Raises	47
Straight Leg Raise	48
Glute/Hamstring Raises	49
Squatted Calf Raises	50
Dragon Flag	51
Lunges	52
Side Lunges	53
Crossover Lunges	54
Alternating Plyometric Lunge	55
Walking Lunges	56
Reverse Lunge with Front Kick	57
Jumping Lunge	58
Corkscrew Lunge	59

Chapter 3: Crunches, Alternatives to Deadlifts and Other Exercises .. 61
    Sit Up 62
    Twisting Crunches 63
    Crunches 64
    Advanced Crunch 65
    Bicycle Crunch 66
    One Legged Calf Raise 67
    Basic Calf Raise 68
    Scissor Kicks 69
    Hyperextensions 70
    Short Back Bridge 71
    Full Bridge 72
    Step Ups 73
    V-Ups 74
    Pulse Up 75
    Upside Down Shoulder Press 76
    Jumping Jacks 77
    Double Pulse Jump Squats 78
    Squat Jumps 79
    Broad Jump 80
    Hockey Squat Jumps 81
    Box Jump 82
    Jump Squat on a Step 83
    Plank 84
    Plank with Leg Raise 85
    Two Point Plank 86
    Side Plank 87
    Knee to Elbow Planks 88
    Spider Plank 89
    Reverse Plank with Leg Lift 90
    Rotational Reach 91

Burpee	92
Hanging Oblique Raises	93
Windshield Wipers	94
Mountain Climber	95
Bench Knee Pull in	96
Superwoman	97
Tabletop to Reverse Pike	98
Glute Bridge March	99
Neck Extension	100
Neck Side Turn	101
Neck Glide Retraction	102
Reverse Crunch	103
Toe Touch Crunches	104
Russian Twist	105
One Legged Bodyweight Deadlift	106
Commando Pull Ups	107
Pseudo Planche Push Ups	108
Stretches	109
Fold over Stretch	110
Triceps Stretch	111
The Quad Stretch	112
The Swan Stretch	113
Calisthenics Training Tips	115
Conclusion	117
A Word from the Author	118

Introduction

Many people love the attractive physique that they can achieve after spending months in the gym lifting weights. What you may not realize is that you can still achieve the same results, without having to do any heavy lifting. With Calisthenics, you will focus on sculpting and building your muscles even when there are limited machines or weights available. This is because you will be using resistance through several exercises that capitalize on your body weight for added pressure.

This book contains bodyweight exercises that will literally work out muscles on your entire body, giving you an enviable chiseled look. You will find that the more you do these exercises the easier they will become. When you just start out, they will be slightly challenging.

Take control of your physique and overall health, and use bodyweight to get the right results. Here are 108 ways that will help you.

CHAPTER 1

Push Ups, Pull Ups and Squats

This book begins with the most well-known Calisthenics exercises, and these exercises are able to build your upper body muscles as well as your lower body muscles. As you do these exercises, you need to remember that it is important to breathe in deeply, and always hold your abdominal muscles rigid through the exercise.

It is up to you how many repetitions that you will do for each exercise, based on your level of fitness. It is recommended that a set of eight for each exercise (on each side of the body if relevant) is ideal for your workout. Use these exercises and create your own customized workout so that you can get the results you are looking for.

Basic Push-Up

A

B

To do a push up, begin by lying down in the plank position. Your hands should be on the ground right underneath your shoulders. Keep your balance by using your toes and tighten your abs. Keep your back flat and lower your body until your chest is close to the floor. Use the strength in your arms to push yourself back up.

Decline Push Up

Lie on the floor face down. Place your hands apart as you hold your torso up at arm's length. Place your legs on a bench, or a stair or a box. Your body should be in a straight line. Lower your body downwards until your chest is almost touching the floor. Do this as you inhale. Now lift your body slowly to the starting position as you breathe out, squeezing your chest. Take a moment before you lower yourself down again.

Incline Push Up

Get a bench or a box. Place your hands on the edge of the box or bench ensuring that they are slightly wider than your shoulder length. Position your feet back from the bench, and keep your body straight. Lower your chest to the edge of the bench or box by bending your arms. Slowly push your body up to the former position. This completes a rep.

Clapping Push Up

Begin by getting into the basic push up position, keeping your hands place outside your shoulders. Go down into a push up and the push your upper body up off the ground. While you are in the air, do a quick clap and then get your hands back into the push up position for landing.

Crossover Push Up

STEP 1 STEP 2 STEP 3

STEP 4 STEP 5

This pushup will help build your upper body strength, especially your arms and your core. Start in the push up position. Place your left arm on the step and go down into the pushup. Go back up and place both bands on the step. Put your left arm down and do another push up.

Knee Push Ups

Get into the standard push up position and place your arms a little further than shoulder width apart. Cross your legs at your knees and ankles and then by bending your elbows, lower your weight and when your elbows are at a 90-degree angle hold the position and then push yourself back up.

Diamond Push Up

Begin by getting into the standard push up position and then place your hands together right under your chest such that your thumbs and your index fingers are touching forming the shape of a diamond. For balance, keep your feet apart and slowly push your body up and down.

Handstand Push Up

To do this advanced push up, begin by facing the wall and keeping a standing position. Then, kick up your feet so that you are in a handstand position. Hold in your abs and tighten your thighs and glutes. Lower yourself to the ground by bending your elbows at a 90-degree angle. Hold the position, and then push yourself back up.

Spider Push Up

To do this exercise, begin by getting into a standard push up position. When you are lowering your body, life up a knee and get it to touch your elbow. As you push back up, return your leg into the starting position. Repeat with the other leg.

Dolphin Push Up

This is an excellent exercise for working out your core muscles and building strength. To do this exercise, start by getting into the pushup pose, ensuring that your weight is being supported by your toes and elbows. Push your behind right up into the air so that your body forms an upside down V. Bring your body back into the starting position, while raising your head up and ensuring that your arms are outstretched.

Single Leg Push Up

To perform a single leg push up, begin by getting into the standard push up position. Raise one foot off the ground and, while tightening your core, lower your body until your elbow makes an angle of 90°. Return to the starting position to complete the exercise. It is important to remember to keep your back and leg straight as you do this exercise.

CALISTHENICS

Push Up with Reach

To do a push up with reach, first get into the standard press up position. Then, as you lower yourself to perform the press up, move one hand forward until you lock your elbow straight. Switch arms with every repetition. You may use slide boards or Val slides to make this exercise a little easier.

Staggered Push Ups

To perform a staggered push up, first get into the classic push up position, but move one hand further forward than the other hand. Perform a press up as normal with your hands in this position. Switch hands at the end of the set.

Superman Pushup

This is an excellent exercise for working the whole body, and is amongst the most challenging Calisthenics exercises you can try. Start out this exercise by lying down flat on the ground ensuring that both your legs and your arms are fully outstretched. Push your body up and then lift it, ensuring that you raise your whole body several inches off the ground. Go back to the starting position and repeat.

Pull Ups

For this exercise, you can choose between a wide grip, a medium grip and a close grip. Grab the pull up bar with your arms facing forward and pull yourself up. Your arms should be extended in front of you, holding the bar, with your chest pushed out. Start in this position. Now pull your torso up until your chest is touching the pull up bar. This should be done while you are exhaling. After a second in that position, start inhaling as you lower your body down to the starting position.

Sternum Pull Up

Get into the normal starting position for pull ups, holding on to the pull bar and hanging with your ankles loosely crossed behind you. Your palm should be facing backwards. With an intense amount of power, pull yourself as far as you can, tilting your head back so that your chest touches the bar in the lowest possible position. Lower yourself back down.

Inclined Pull Up

Begin by lying down and holding on to the bar, keeping your hands just over a shoulder width apart. Your grip should be overhand. Balance your weight with your arms. Keeping your feet straight so that just your heels are touching the floor. Pull yourself up until your head is elevated over the bar, hold the position and then lower yourself back down.

Side to Side Pull Up

Begin this exercise by standing before a chin bar, holding on to the bar with your palms forward and back curved slightly. Lift your body up and move to your left side. While you do this, bring your chin to the bar and hold. Move back down and repeat the same movement on the other side.

Muscle Up

Begin this exercise in a standard pull up position hanging from the bar. Begin by swinging out your feet so that your body gains some momentum and then pull yourself all the way over the bar so that your chest is above the bar. Hold the position and then lower yourself back down again.

Shoulder Width Chin Up

With your palms facing you, grab the chin up bar. Keep your hands shoulder width apart. Hang with your hands straight and your legs crossed at the ankle. This is the starting position. Start by squeezing your shoulder blades close together as you pull your chest towards the bar. Your shoulders and your neck should be relaxed all this time. Return slowly to the starting position by lowering your chest from the bar until your hands are fully extended.

Towel Grip Pull Up

To perform this exercise, hang two towels over the pull up bar, separating them by your shoulder width. Then grasping the towels as high up as you possibly can, raise your body up until your torso touches the pull up bar as it would during a regular pull up, and lower yourself down to complete one rep. When performing this exercise, it is important to use a towel that is thick, so that it will not tear. If you are trying this exercise in the gym, remember gym towels are pretty thin, so you should use a couple of them.

CALISTHENICS

One Arm Chin Up

To perform this exercise, first grab the pull up bar with your right hand using the standard chin-up grip (palms facing you), and hold your left hand behind your back. Next, raise your right hip to shorten the distance between it and your right shoulder. Finally, pull yourself up until your chin is above the bar, making sure you use your core and lats, not your arm. Lower yourself down slowly to complete the exercise. Remember to switch arms at the end of every set.

The Human Flag

This is the most challenging type of pull up that you can try as it requires a considerable amount of strength to hold the position. Youi will work out the muscles that are on your arms, shoulders and wrists, as well as your abdominals. To do this exercise, hold on to a standing pole with your arms and then raise your legs in a fluid movement until you are in the position of a flag. Hold for as long as you can manage and repeat.

Squats

Stand straight with your feet at about shoulder length apart. Your toes should be pointed outwards to maintain body stability. Place your arms behind your head. Push your hips back and slowly bend your knees up to about 90 degrees. Continue going down until your hamstrings are parallel to the floor. Do not allow your knees to go beyond the tips of your toes. Let your body weight lie on your heels. Pause in that position for a second, then slowly rise up to the starting position.

Wall Squats

Stand up straight ensuring that your feet are shoulder-width apart. Keep your back straight against the exercise ball. Cross your arms in front of you. Slowly slide your back against the wall until you seem to be seated at an imaginary chair. Bend until your knees are at about 90 degrees. Hold on that position for a few seconds, with your thighs parallel to the ground and your back straight. Stay in that position for a few seconds, then slowly go back to the starting point.

Pistol Squats

To perform a pistol squat, stand straight with your arms extended ahead of you, keeping your elbows straight. Hold your non-working leg straight in front of you, and slowly lower yourself to the ground. Unlike the regular one leg squat, with the pistol squat you have to lower yourself all the way to the ground until your hamstring touches your calf and your knee is over your toes. You must also keep your non-working leg parallel to the ground when you get to the bottom of the squat. Return to the standing position to complete the exercise.

Pile Squats

Start by standing straight with your legs wider apart than your shoulder length. Your toes should be pointing outwards. Place your hands on your hips. Slowly lower yourself to a sitting position. Pause in that position for a second, then slowly go back to the starting position.

One Legged Squat

To start this exercise, stand up straight, stretch your arms out in front of you keeping your elbows straight and then extend one foot forward in front of you, keeping it straight as well. Slowly lower yourself into the squat position placing your weight on the leg that is touching the ground. Return to the starting position and repeat on the other side.

Eagle Squats

This is a rather tricky exercise and needs a lot of balance to execute. To perform this exercise, wrap your right foot around your left calf, and your right hand around your left forearm until your hands are together. Once you are in this position, lower yourself as far as you can and hold for a few seconds, and return to the starting position.

Sumo Squat

To do this, start by standing with your legs apart and bringing your hands together in front of you. Lower yourself down to work out your inner this. Raise your heel on one leg to work your calf muscle, and then switch and do the same with the other leg. Return to the standing position.

Figure Four Squat

To execute a Figure Four Squat, begin in a standing position. Bend your knees to lower yourself into a semi-squat, and cross your right leg over your left leg. Taking care to maintain your balance, complete the squat by lowering yourself until your left thigh is parallel to the ground. Return to the standing position and switch legs.

Squat Jacks

To do a Squat Jack, stand with your feet close together and do a squat. When you get to the lowest part of your squat, hold your position. Now do a squat jump, but stay low in the squat position and separate your legs in the process, as if you were doing a jumping jack. Jump again to bring your feet back together. It is important that you do not return to the standing position until you have completed your set.

CHAPTER 2

Dips, Raises and Lunges

The next exercises contained in this section will work your entire body, particularly building up your arms and your legs. They include the following: -

Dips

This will work out your triceps. Start by sitting on a bench. Using your feet, move yourself forward until you are in the sitting position, your hands supporting your body, but you are no longer sitting on the bench. Then, slowly lower your body ensuring that your forearms remain straight and your elbows are bent. When you reach a 90-degree angle, stop, and then push yourself back up until you are in the sitting position.

Chest Dips on a Straight Bar

This exercise is excellent for building your upper body and will help to strengthen your triceps, anterior deltoids and pectorals. It can easily be done between two chairs if you do not have the straight bars where you work out. You should begin by grabbing hold of the dip bars, and jump up. Ensure that your arms are straight and bend your knees gently. Slowly lower your body until your shoulders are lower than your elbows. Lean forward to maintain your balance.

Bench Dips

This is a great way to start building up your triceps. Place your feet on one bench and balance your upper body using the other bench. Keeping your arms rigid, bend them at the elbows and slowly lower your body to a 90-degree angle. Hold the position for several seconds and the get back into the starting position.

Dip to Leg Raisers

This exercise may seem simple but is much harder to execute than it seems. To execute a Dip to Leg raiser, first grab hold of either parallel dip bars or two chairs, and perform a standard dip. However, when you are raising yourself up, begin to swing your legs forward so that when you are at the top of the motion your legs are stretched out in front of you. Hold the position for a few seconds, then lower your legs to complete the exercise. This exercise is especially good for your chest and abs.

Incline Dip

The Incline dip is a very good exercise for building your chest and triceps while reducing the risk of inuring your shoulders. To execute an Incline Dip, hold the parallel bars and lift yourself off the ground. While doing so, raise your knees towards your chest so that your thighs are parallel to the ground (like you are sitting in a chair). You will need to hold them at this angle for the rest of the exercise. Lower yourself down until your upper arms are parallel to the ground and your elbows have bent 90°, allowing your upper body to swing forward to maintain balance. Hold this position for a few seconds then return to the starting position.

One Arm Triceps Dips

This is a more challenging variation to the standard dip. To perform this exercise, first enter the classic dip position, with your arms on a bench or a chair supporting your body in a sitting position. Then, lift your right arm and left leg so that they are parallel with the ground, and you are only resting on your left arm and right leg. From this position, lower yourself until your elbow is at a 90° angle, keeping your extended arm and leg straight in the process. Raise yourself back up to complete the exercise, and switch to the opposite position at the end of the set. If you would like to challenge yourself, you could switch legs after every rep, almost like a Russian Cossack dancer. This should help exercise your abs as well.

Wall Sit

Stand straight against a wall. Keep your feet about 2 feet away from the wall. Slightly spread your feet. Slowly slide your back against the wall bending your knees to about 90 degrees. Maintain a sitting position, with your thighs parallel to the floor. Stay in that position for about 3o seconds then slowly rise back to the starting position.

Leg Raises

Start by hanging straight from a pull up bar. Raise your legs until they are at a 90-degree angle at the waist. Try to push your abdominal muscles towards your spine. Hold in position for a few seconds then slowly go back to the starting point.

Lying Leg Raises

Lie down with your back straight and legs straight. Keep your hands on the sides, holding the bench. This is the starting position. Raise your legs slowly until they make a 90-degree angle from the waist. Keep your knees straight. Hold that position then slowly return to the starting position.

Lying Torso Raises

Lie on the floor, with your face down. Loosely place your hands on your sides with your palms facing down. This is the starting position. Slowly raise your torso until your chest is off the ground and then extend your neck back as you look at the ceiling. This should contract your lower back muscles. Hold for a few seconds, then slowly go back in the starting position.

Lying Side Leg Raises

Begin this exercise by lying down on your side. Use one arm to support your head and place the other arm, palm down in front of you. Extend both eggs out keeping the straight. Lift one leg up towards the ceiling keeping your toes pointed until you reach a 90-degree angle. Repeat several times. Turn and repeat on the other side.

Side Leg Raises

Lie down on your side for the starting position. Place your head on your arm, keeping it folded so that your head rests on the crook near your elbow. Keep the other hand placed on the ground, palm down. Your legs should be straight. Slowly raise your leg up until you reach a 60-degree angle. Hold, and then lower it down. Repeat on the other side.

Straight Leg Raise

Start this exercise by lying down flat on yo0ur back. You should place a rolled towel under your neck for support. Keep your arms straight at your sides. Without bending your knees, lift one leg until you can see your toes. Hold for a moment and lower. Repeat with the other leg.

Glute/Hamstring Raises

To perform this exercise, you will need a partner or somewhere you can brace your feet. Begin by getting onto your knees, keeping your upper legs and upper body upright. Lower your body by leaning forward, making sure that you keep your body straight and restrict hip movement. Put your hands in front of you as you near the bottom of the movement, and slowly push yourself off the floor to help you return to the start position.

Squatted Calf Raises

This is another interesting variation to a popular exercise that targets your whole lower body, from your glutes to your calves. To perform this exercise, lower yourself into the standard squatting position, then, while keeping your back straight, lift your heels until you are standing on your toes. Hold the position for a few seconds, then return to the squatting position. Remember not to return to the standing position until you have completed one set.

Dragon Flag

This move was invented by Bruce Lee, and is a very tricky maneuver to execute, therefore, you should only attempt it after you have been exercising for a while and gained some core strength. Form is also very important if you want to avoid injury, so ensure that when you are doing this exercise you leave no weight on your vertebrae.

To begin, lie down on your back on a bench, or the floor, ensuring that you have something behind your head to grab on to for support. Raise your legs, glutes and lower back into the air, leaving only your head and shoulders on the ground or bench. While keeping your body in a straight line, and resisting gravity, lower your body back down as slowly as possible. Once you feel the need to increase the challenge, do not allow your legs to touch the ground, but lift them back up just before to increase the work your core is doing.

Lunges

Stand up with a straight upper body, chin up, eyes right ahead and your shoulders back and relaxed, step one foot forward. Lower your hips a little until both of your knees are bent at about 90 degrees. Ensure that your front knee is at least directly above your ankle and that your other knee is not touching the ground. Rest your body weight on your heels and pause there for a second before you push yourself back to the starting position.

Side Lunges

Stand up straight, with knees and hips slightly bent. Your feet should be shoulder-width apart. Keep your head and chest up. Start with this position. Take a small step to the right and keep your toes pointed outwards. Slide your left leg and extend your left knee while you push your body weight to the right. Hold this position. Change the legs after a few seconds.

Crossover Lunges

Get to the starting position of a basic lunge. Cross your left leg over the right leg and try to lunge as far as you can to the right side as you land on your heel. Change the legs over to do the other side. This can be easier if you do it with a walking forward motion.

Alternating Plyometric Lunge

This is a great exercise to work on your quads and groin, and also build your glutes and hamstrings. Begin by standing up with your feet shoulder width apart. Then, once you are in a complete lunge and your knee is close to the ground, jump back with force and change your leg positions while you are in the air. When you land, return to the lunge position. Repeat this several times to create a set. Remember to keep your arms straight and rigid and balled into fists.

Walking Lunges

This exercise begins with you standing up straight with your hands on your hips. Step forward and lower your hips as if you are doing a standard lunge, however, instead of moving back to the original starting position when you are coming back up, move your back foot forward so that you end up ahead of where you started. Repeat the process for the opposing foot.

Reverse Lunge with Front Kick

Begin by standing upright with your feet a shoulder width apart. Take one step back and then bend your knees until you are in the lunge position, keeping your arms up and bent at the elbow. Launch into a front kick, by extending the foot that is bent behind you upwards and kick as high as you can. Go back into start position and repeat with the other leg.

Jumping Lunge

Start this exercise by standing up straight and tall, and from this position, into a lunge. After the lunge, push yourself off from your feet and the bottom and jump. While you are in the jump switch up your legs and then land and return into the lunge position.

Corkscrew Lunge

This exercise is a great way to work out your abs and your lower body at the same time. To perform a Corkscrew Lunge, stand up straight with your hands behind your head and perform an ordinary lunge by placing your right foot in front of you and lowering your hips until both of your knees are at a 90° angle with the ground. While you are doing this, twist your upper body, bringing your left elbow towards your right knee. Return to the starting position, and repeat the lunge again, this time changing the leading leg.

CHAPTER 3

Crunches, Alternatives to Deadlifts and Other Exercises

This chapter contains crunches and alternatives to deadlifts to build y0ur muscles as well as an assortment of exercises that are more complex to master.

Sit Up

Lie down on the floor keeping your body straight. Bend your legs at your knees. Lock your hands behind your head to finish the starting position. Now slowly lift your upper body until it is forming a V-shape with your thighs as you slowly breathe out. Hold for a few seconds and then lower your body slowly to the starting position as you inhale.

Twisting Crunches

Lie down flat on your back with your knees bent. Place your hands on the back of your head. This is the starting position. Raise your torso and twist your waist, keeping your elbow in the air. Return to the starting position, and then repeat on the other side.

Crunches

Lie flat on your back with your knees bent and your arms crossed on your chest. Your feet should be about 4 inches apart, with your toes pointing inwards, touching the ground. Slowly lift your shoulders off the ground as you push your lower back down. Do this as you exhale. Stay in that contraction position for a second or two, then go back slowly to the starting position as you inhale.

Advanced Crunch

Get into the crunch position as normal with your hands behind your heat and your knees slightly bent while lying on your back. Slowly life your shoulders off the ground and as you do so, raise your legs as well so that your toes are pointing towards the ceiling. Hold this position for a few minutes and then return to the starting position.

Bicycle Crunch

Lie flat on the floor, with your feet and hands stretched out. Place your hands on the back of your head and interlock your fingers. Raise your legs to the point where your thighs are perpendicular to the ground. Try to touch your right elbow to your left knee while raising your knee to the elbow. While doing this, leave the other leg straight but slightly raised from the ground. Switch to the other side and repeat several times.

One Legged Calf Raise

Stand in an upright position with your hands on your hips. Place a weight on the ground and put one foot on the weight. Now slowly lift the other leg to the back by bending the knee. This is the start position. Extend your ankle as much as possible in order to raise your heel at the toes, then stand on your tip toes. Repeat this and then change your legs over.

Basic Calf Raise

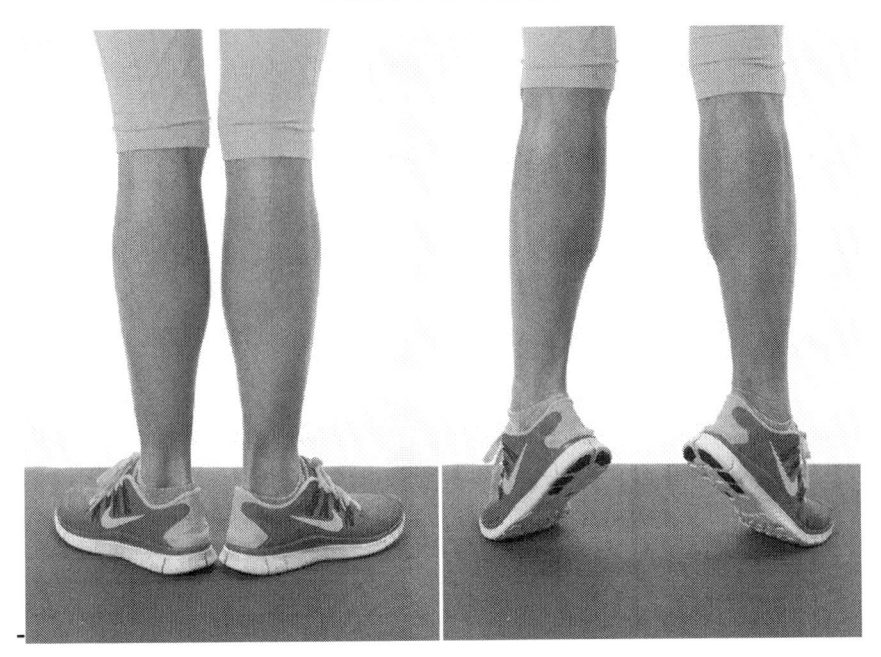

This is probably one of the easiest, yet most effective exercises there is. To perform a basic calf raise, stand with your feet close together, and slowly raise your heels off the ground until you are standing on your toes. Hold the position for a few seconds, then slowly lower yourself back down. It is important not to bounce or bend your knees during this exercise so that you can get the most out of it.

CALISTHENICS

Scissor Kicks

A

B

Lie down on an exercise mat. Extend your hands to the sides with your palms face down. Keep your knees straight and then lift your legs slowly and maintain a starting position where your heels are about 6 inches from the ground. Your hands should stay in the same position throughout the exercise. Now slowly lift one leg further to about 45 degrees while the other leg stays in the starting position. Switch the legs as you breathe in and out deeply.

Hyperextensions

Lie on a hyperextension bench with your face down. Tuck your ankles on the machine's footpads. Let your upper thighs rest comfortably across the wide. Keep your body straight then fold your arms on your chest. This will be the starting position. Slowly bend forward and stretch your waist as far as possible, while keeping your back flat all the while. Continue moving forward as you inhale until you can no longer move forward. Now raise your torso in order to go back to the starting position as you exhale.

Short Back Bridge

This is a fantastic alternative to a dead lift, and will help to exercise your lower back, especially if you have a previous injury. To do perform a short back bridge, lie on your back and bend your knees. Raise your glutes and your core off the ground as high as you can, keeping your shoulders on the ground. Hold for a couple of seconds and return to the start position. Remember to keep your glutes and your core tight as you perform this exercise.

Full Bridge

To perform the Full Bridge, lie on your back with your knees bent and your hands beside your head, fingers pointing towards your feet. Raise your glutes and your core off the ground, and push your shoulders off the ground curving your back as you do so. At this point, the only parts of your body that should be touching the ground are your hands and feet. Hold for a few seconds and return to the starting position.

CALISTHENICS

Step Ups

Beginning in a standing position, place your left foot on the step. Take a step by straightening your right leg and raising your left leg, bending it at the knee to a 90-degree angle. Return to the starting position, stepping one foot down at a time until you have two feet on the floor. Repeat with the right leg.

V-Ups

Lie flat on the ground and ensure that your back is pressed firmly on the ground. Extend both of your arms and extend your legs so that your body makes a straight line. Ensure that the back of your shoulders are touching the floor and your palms are facing the roof. Your feet should be together and your toes should be facing the roof as well. Lift your legs up together as you keep them straight. Slowly lift your torso as you try to reach your toes with your hands keeping the elbows straight. Slowly return to the starting position and repeat.

Pulse Up

This is the perfect exercise for your abs. Lie flat on your back. Lift your legs up and without bending your knees point them straight up towards the ceiling. Keep your arms flat on your side with your palms down. Raise your hips until they are no longer on the ground without swinging your legs. Hold the position, and then lower your hips back down, returning to the position at the start.

Upside Down Shoulder Press

Start in the pushup position, and then using your knees, elevate your lower back while keeping your palms on the ground. Imagine that someone is pulling your belly button through you from your back. When you get into position, slowly lower your upper body by bending your elbows until your heat almost touches the ground. For balance, you should stand on your tip toes.

Jumping Jacks

Stand straight with your feet together and your hands stretched down by your side. Quickly jump up and separate your legs so that they are just over shoulder width apart at the same time raise your hands up above your head. Reverse this motion and repeat as required.

Double Pulse Jump Squats

Stand straight with your feet at shoulder-width apart and your arms stretched outwards. Go down and complete a squat and pause at the bottom for a few seconds. Now start pulsing up and down a few inches and going back to the position. You can then pulse and jump alternatively a few times before you rise up to the starting position. Repeat as required.

Squat Jumps

A   **B**

Stand straight and put your feet at shoulder width apart. Get into the basic squat position. Now, jump in the air and on landing back, return to the squat position to finish one rep. You have to maintain balance for an effective squat jump.

Broad Jump

This exercise will work out the muscles in your legs including the quads, hamstrings and hip flexors. Start by standing with your feet apart with your arms in the air. Push your arms back behind you as your bend your knees. Your hips should be pushed back as well. Then swing your arms forward and go into a high jump. As you land, bend your body back into the starting position. Repeat as you wish.

Hockey Squat Jumps

Stand straight, with your legs slightly wide apart and your hands on the back of your head. Go down to complete a squat and hold in that position for a few seconds. Now jump explosively until your entire body weight is resting on your toes and your hands are still at the back of your head. Go down to the starting position and repeat this exercise a few more times.

Box Jump

Begin with a platform in front of you and stand around six inches behind it. Get into the squat position with your arms extended behind you. Explore upward and jump, so that you land on the box. Once you do, get back into a position where your knees are bent. Jump off the box again to complete a rep.

Jump Squat on a Step

Stand in front of a step or a box. With your legs at shoulder-length apart, go down slowly to make a squat and pause slightly above the chair or box. Now jump explosively up then back and land on the step. Without losing balance or sitting on the step, return into the squat position.

Plank

This exercise will work your abs as well as your shoulders and lower back. Begin in the basic push up position. Shift your weight so that it is resting on your elbows and forearms instead of on your hands. With your hips raised from the ground, keep your body in a straight line and hold this position, first for thirty seconds and then for longer. Remember to breathe deeply.

Plank with Leg Raise

Start this exercise by getting into the plank position and hold for several seconds. Slowly. Raise your left leg up, bending it at the knee slightly. Hold for a few seconds and return to the plank position. Repeat with the other leg

Two Point Plank

Begin this exercise by getting into the plank position, except instead of resting your weight on your forearms, you will elevate your body with your palms down and arms straight. Keep your feet a distance apart. This is the position to start in. Then, stretch your right arm forward while raising your left leg simultaneously keeping both straight as you hold the position. Return to the starting position and repeat with the other side.

Side Plank

This exercise will work your oblique muscles and abs. Start by lying down on your left side and place your feet together. Using your left elbow stretching to your forearm as a prop, raise your hips ensuring that body is in a straight line. For balance, put your right hand onto your right hip and hold the position. Change sides.

Knee to Elbow Planks

Get into the plank position and hold for a few seconds. Slowly bring your left knee up to your elbow as far as it can reach. Hold and return to the starting plank position. Repeat with the other leg.

CALISTHENICS

Spider Plank

To do this exercise, start in the push up position, holding your body still so that it forms a straight position like the plank. Then, with your arms straight bend your left knee bringing it to touch your left elbow. Hold this position for s few seconds, return to the starting position and repeat with the right leg and right elbow.

Reverse Plank with Leg Lift

With this reverse plank where instead of being face down you are face up. Using your arms for support, get into the reverse plank position ensuring your legs are together and your body makes a straight line. Hold this position. Slowly raise one leg to as close to a 90-degree angle as you can reach. Hold the position. Lower and repeat with the other leg.

CALISTHENICS

Rotational Reach

Begin in the starting push up position. Once you have your balance, and keeping your arms straight, extend your right arm out, pointing it towards the ceiling. Rotate using your entire body and move your neck so that it is looking at the ceiling as well. Hold and exchange sides.

Burpee

This exercise will work out muscles all over your body (except for your neck). Begin in a standing position with your feet a hip width apart and your arms on your sides. Then bend your knees and lower your hips while placing your hands in front of you and touching the ground. Next, kick your feet back so that you are in the push up position. Pull your feet back in with your knees wide apart and your hands between them touching the ground. Finish by jumping up with your hands reaching into the air.

Hanging Oblique Raises

Start this exercise by handing from a pull up bar using a grip which is overhand. Then, bend your knees and lift your hips upwards, so that they are at a 90-degree angle with your waist. Swing slightly bringing your right hip to your right hand. Return to the starting position, and then repeat with the other side.

Windshield Wipers

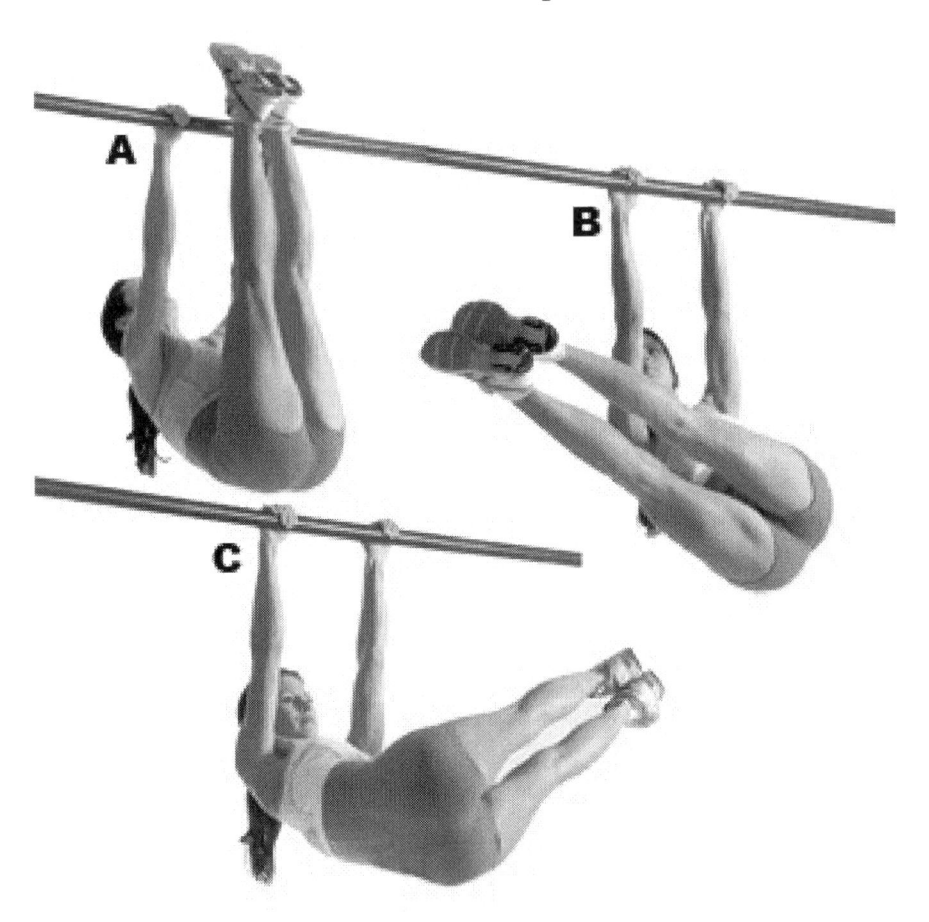

Start by handing off the pull up bar. Slowly raise your legs so that your feet are above the bar and perpendicular to the floor. Your body should be in an L-position. Then, move your legs in swinging motion to the left side, hold for a few minutes and then swing your body again to the right side.

Mountain Climber

This will work almost all the muscles in the body. Start in a basic push up position. Keep your arms straight a shoulder width apart and keep your arms straight. With your body straight. Lift your right foot and bring your knee closer to your chest while holding the position. Put your foot back into the starting position and repeat this with your other leg. Go back and forth.

Bench Knee Pull in

Start by sitting on the bench and then stretching your feet in front of you keeping them straight. Lean back while holding in your abdominals. Bend your knees and bring them up towards your chest. Hold for a few seconds and return to the starting position.

CALISTHENICS

Superwoman

This exercise commences with your lying down on your stomach completely flat. Hold in your abs and stretch yours arms out before. Imagine you are flying by raising your arms and legs, and then lifting your chest from the floor. Hold this position, and release to the starting one. This is one rep.

Tabletop to Reverse Pike

To begin this exercise, you should sit down with your hands down by your sides palm down. Then your knees and using your heels, lift up your hips from the ground. Keep your arms straight and use your feet and hands for support. Hold this position for a few seconds. Keeping your arms straight, straighten your legs as you lower your hips and stop when your hips are just above the flow. Use your abdominal muscles to support you.

Glute Bridge March

Begin by lying down on your back, with your arms palm down by your sides. Raise both your knees and keep your feet firmly on the ground. Then raise your left knee keeping it straight. Use your arms for balance ad raise your hips upwards until your body is in a straight line and hold. Lower yourself to the starting position and repeat with the other leg.

Neck Extension

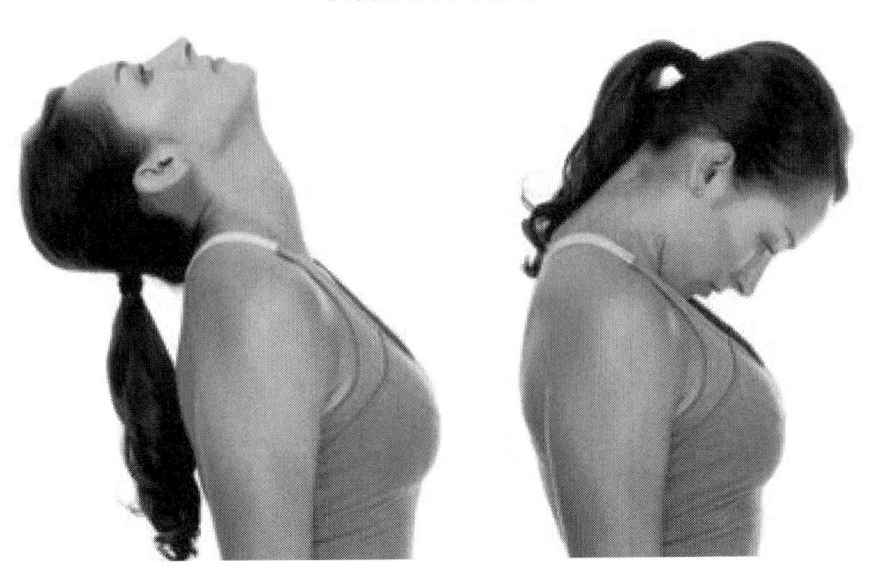

Begin by looking straight ahead and then tilt your head back as far as you can go. Hold this position for a few seconds. Then move your head forward as far as you can go. Hold and then return to the starting position.

Neck Side Turn

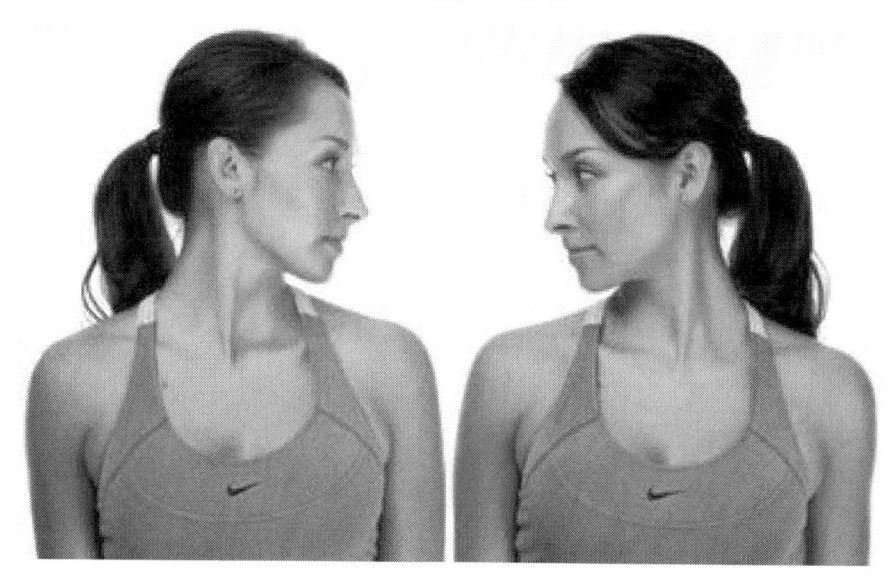

Start this exercise by looking straight ahead. Then turn to the left side as far as you can go. Hold this position for a few seconds. Return to the starting position and then turn your head to the right side as far as you can go. Return to the starting position.

Neck Glide Retraction

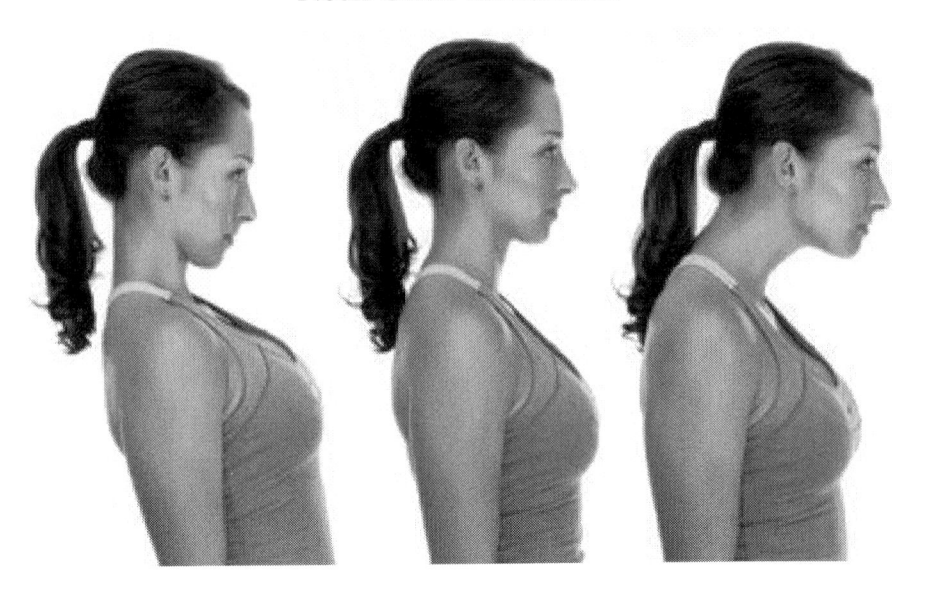

Begin in the starting position and then lean back using your neck. Return to the starting position and push your face forward using your neck.

Reverse Crunch

This is a basically the reverse of the normal crunch, and it is your lower body that moves, not your upper body. To carry out a reverse crunch, begin by lying on your back with your legs raised and your calves parallel to the ground. Then, with your arms beside you, and raise your butt and lower back off the ground, using just your lower abdominals to achieve the effect. Slowly, lower your back to the ground to complete the exercise.

Toe Touch Crunches

The Toe Touch crunch is a simplified version of the V up, and works out your whole core. To do a Toe Touch crunch, get into the standard crunch position, stretch your arms behind you and raise your legs so that they are pointing straight into the air. Swing your arms forward, raising your shoulders off the floor and reach for your toes. Swing your legs towards your fingers a little bit while keeping them straight as you do so. Hold the position for a second before slowly lowering your body back to the start position.

Russian Twist

The Russian twist is a good exercise for your core, and demands balance and coordination. To perform a Russian Twist, sit on the floor and lean back a little so that you are at an angle, and lift your feet off the floor, keeping your knees at a 45° angle. Next, twist your body to the right, keeping your feet in the air and your knees bent. Hold this position for a few seconds before twisting in the other direction. Remember to keep your core tight throughout the exercise to ensure that you gain the full benefits.

One Legged Bodyweight Deadlift

This is a fantastic alternative to the traditional weighted deadlift, and it works almost the whole body, focusing on the hamstrings, lower back and glutes. To perform the One Legged Deadlift, begin in a standing position, with your feet about shoulder width apart. Slowly lean your body forward, keeping your back straight and sticking one leg behind you. You should lower your arms as well to help maintain balance. At the bottom of the move, your back and leg should form a straight line that is parallel to the ground, while your arms should be at a 90° angle to the ground. Hold that position for a few seconds and slowly return to the starting position to complete the exercise. Once you have completed a set, switch legs and repeat.

Commando Pull Ups

Commando pull ups are some of the best exercises for the chest, arms, and upper back, and are more difficult than they appear. To perform a Commando pull up, first hold the pull up bar with an overhand grip with one hand, and an underhand grip with the other. Then, pull your body up using your chest, and keep your head to one side of the bar at the peak. Lower your body, and pull up again, this time pulling your head to the other side of the bar. Once you are done with one set, switch your hand grip and repeat the exercise.

Pseudo Planche Push Ups

These are some of the most taxing pushups you will ever perform, and they are designed to work your whole upper body. To perform a Pseudo Planche push up, begin by getting into the standard push up position, but lean forward so that your hands are in line with your hips, and point your hands and your elbows backwards. Lower your body as with a normal push up, making sure that you keep your back straight and your core engaged, and that you maintain the lean as you descend. Push yourself slowly back up to the start position to complete one rep.

Stretches

Calisthenics are excellent exercises if you are motivated to tone and strengthen your entire body so that you have a stunning silhouette. However, this is only possible if your muscles are in the best shape possible, which happens when you take the time to carry out stretches. Here are some stretches that you need to include at the beginning and the end of your workout. You deserve the best results, so do as much as you can right.

Fold over Stretch

To do this stretch, begin by standing up straight keeping your feet apart a hip width. Breathe out and bend yourself forward at the waist, slowly, lowering your head until it is between your knees. Hold the position for as long as you can. To get back into the standing position, bend your knees and come up slowly.

Triceps Stretch

In a standing or sitting upright position, extend your arms above your head. Take your right hand and bend it at the elbow, such that the palm of that hand reaches towards your upper back. Then, take your left hand and use it to hold the right elbow. Draw the elbow back moving closer to your head and hold the position for thirty seconds. Repeat with the other arm.

The Quad Stretch

For this exercise, you should kneel down on the floor ensuring that your shins are both down. Then, take your right leg and lunge it in front of you, ensuring that your knee is at a 90 degree angle. Keep your foot flat on the floor, place both your hands onto your right knee and then push your back him frontward. You will feel a stretch in your hips and quads. Hold for half a minute, and release. Repeat several times and switch legs.

The Swan Stretch

Begin by lying face down with your hands in front of your shoulders, making sure that your fingers are facing forward, and that your legs are outstretched behind you. Now, use your hands by pressing them down and lift your mid-section off the ground. Hold in your abs. Keep your shoulders down, straighten your upper body and tilt your head back to open up your chest. Hold the position for at least one minute.

So how else will you benefit from these stretches? Here are the additional advantages: -

1. Save yourself from getting hurt or experiencing pain. By stretching, you are easing possible pressure that may have built up in your joints which would limit the way that your body can move as

you exercise. In addition, warming yourself up prevents strain and pain that could occur in your body.

2. Your circulation will become so much better, as you encourage your blood to flow all over your body, especially to your muscles. This means that you will be better able to recover from the exercises that you carry out.

3. Stretching also helps to relieve stress in your mind, which could interrupt the way that you are exercising. Being in the right frame of mind will help you make better decisions as you work out.

Calisthenics Training Tips

There are more than eighty exercises included in this book, and it would be impossible for you to do every single one of them at one go. They have varying levels of difficulty and work out different parts of your body. Here are some tips that will make the process of training so much better for you.

Work Your Entire Body

It is possible that you have some problem areas that you want to work on, perhaps you are looking to build up your abdominals or you want to define your biceps. When you are doing calisthenics, do not carry out the exercises that focus on only one area. Do them all, as your entire body will end up evenly and beautifully toned and strengthened.

Create a Workout Plan

Create a workout plan for each day, where you are able to execute a certain amount of exercises within a fixed time period. The number of exercises that you choose should be based on your strength and ability. You are meant to enjoy exercise, so do not push yourself too hard to begin with. As your skill increases, you will be able to do more challenging exercises.

Be Patient

Mastering all of these exercises will take some time, so be patient as you work your body out. Make sure that when you create goals, there are those that are short term, which will help to keep you encouraged and motivated, and then those which are long term, focusing on the body you want to achieve. Ideally, you need to make these exercises a part of your lifestyle, rather than use them to meet some weight or strength goal.

Make Use of Sets

To get excellent results with calisthenics, you should use reps and sets are much as possible. As you become stronger and better at the exercises, push yourself harder by reducing the amount of rest time that you have between the sets. In addition, increase the intensity of the exercises that you are using, by choosing variations that make them much harder.

Take Care of Yourself

Make sure that you are eating an excellent diet so that your efforts can manifest. A balance of carbs, protein and fat is required.

Conclusion

If you have been attempted each and every one of these exercises, you will immediately begin to notice some significant changes in your body. You will feel stronger, your muscles may be burning and you will feel as though you are able to accomplish more than before. Your flexibility will have improved as well, making it easier for you to move.

These exercises also help with your coordination, so that you are able to move different parts of your body at the same time. This can be seen through exercises including the burpees, or those with the pull up bars.

You should also have increased endurance, being able to hold exercises like the plank for a little longer each time. Through this, you will strengthen your core, and all the other muscles that are offering you support.

The best benefit though should be in the form of weight loss, as you will inevitably burn fat while you do these exercises. The benefit of losing fat in this way is that your body will become more toned, so that you have muscle definition that leaves you looking and feeling great.

Take up Calisthenics and make them a permanent part of your daily work out. You will need minimal equipment so you can do them anywhere, and you will have outstanding results. What better way to achieve the physique of your dreams.

A Word from the Author

Congratulations on taking your fitness into your hands by choosing to try out Calisthenics. I started these exercises over ten years ago, as I lived in wine country, where all around me were trees and grapevines, and finding a gym was close to impossible. I wanted to be stronger, so that I could earn more money working with my hands.

It took me around six months before I started to see real results (there were some milestones I passed along the way) and when I realized this was as a result of my efforts, I never looked back.

I encourage you to stick to the journey of learning Calisthenics, and you will not believe the difference that you can bring to your life. I am a humble man from Italy, and these exercises have changed my life. I have been able to share what I do with the world, and encourage others to experience the highest levels of fitness.

Enjoy the journey.

Mario

Free Bonus
2 chapters of:

Style

Developing Chic Taste for Style and Fashion Made Easy

Contents

Introduction 121
Chapter 1: Build a Basic Outfit 122
Chapter 2: Identify Your Personal Style 126

Introduction

Being fashionable and looking great is something that every woman aspires to. It can also be quite intimidating, especially if you do not know where to start in regards to the items to purchase and what you should wear. Even though you have tried to use magazines to copy outfits that you thought were amazing, you may be surprised to find that they are not working for you. This only happens when you do not understand some fundamentals of fashion.

This is a book which will change the game of how you dress, and it will make the daunting subject of fashion very easy for you to comprehend. It is full of tips and tricks that will help you to develop a chic taste, so that wherever you go, people acknowledge you for having excellent style.

Being chic is all about paying close attention to what you are wearing, and how it flatters the body. It is also about ensuring you have key items in your wardrobe and are confident enough to carry yourself with head held high.

Do not worry about changing your entire wardrobe in order to achieve that chic look. This book will help you work with what you have, and let you know which essential items should be added to your wardrobe to keep it chic and classy. Follow the tips that are within this book, and before long, you will be the style example that many others are looking to emulate.

Chapter 1

Build a Basic Outfit

Have you ever wondered how some people appear to have stepped out of the pages of a magazine every time that you see them? They look amazing, with not a hair out of place and amazing clothes on their bodies. There is an expression that you should wear the clothes, and they should not wear you. This book is about how you can achieve this, and develop your own unique and chic taste. As you prepare to delve into fashion, you need to understand the elements of a basic outfit. Here are the things that you need.

Start with a Base

Every outfit begins with a base, which is what your first layer of clothing is called. The base is typically made up of one of two elements. These could be a skirt or trousers at the bottom, with something else on the top, or you could need a dress. There are some factors that you need to consider when choosing your base, and these are as follows: -

- The activities that you are going to carry out for the day. You need to know what you will be doing as this will determine the type of clothes that you need. If you are going out for the evening, you will need something different than if you are going out to exercises.

- Next, you should consider how you want to feel in your clothes. Are you looking to feel comfortable as you get through your errands for the day, professional or confident? This will also help you select the colors and styles that you prefer.

- Keep in mind the weather you are dressing up for and the means that you will use to get from one place to another. You may need to dress in layers if the temperature is cold or wear something light and airy when it is hot. If you are walking, this will determine the type of shoes that you wear, and if you are in getting in and out of a car, you can be a little less practical.

What you choose as your base is where the definition of your style begins, as it is these elements that will stand out the most when you have finished dressing.

Build on Your Base

Once you have your first layer sorted, you can begin to build on it by adding more layers. There are instances when this is not necessary, because the weather does not require it, or your base outfit looks complete as it is. If you do want to add layers, you can choose from a shirt, jackets, blazers, scarves and so on.

There is a strategy that you should use when adding layers. Begin with the items that are as close to your body as possible, and those that are the most fitting. Your layers should become more voluminous as you go along.

When it comes to layers, you can change up your outfits by choosing items which are of varying lengths, different colors and patterns and textures.

Dressing your Feet

Once you have your base and additional layers, the shoes are the next element of your outfit. There are so many different designs and styles to choose from that you should enjoy this part of picking your outfit immensely. When selecting the colors for your shoes, you can choose a color that matches one of the parts of your base outfit, or something in an entirely contrasting color so that it stands out. The shoes that you wear can add the most important element of style to your outfit.

Pick out your Accessories

It is accessories that will give your outfit that final polish that it needs, adding the essential chic taste to your personal style. There are so many different ways that you can accessorize your outfit, including the addition of jewelry, bags, watches, hats and so on. There is a delicate balance between excellent accessorizing and taking it a step too far.

To get this balance right, ensure that you have on accessory which can stand out as a statement piece. This is the one that will draw the attention of any person who is looking at your outfit. You can then add other accessories based on how this works with your overall look.

Once you have put all these elements together, you should be able to put together a great outfit. It is essential that you think through each piece that you are putting on, ensuring that it adds some value to your complete look. Fashion gets messy when you do not take the time to think through your outfit, and instead, simply throw some items on.

Achieving the Chic Look

You do not need to rush out and purchase an entirely new wardrobe so that you can look chic in your clothing. There are several things that you can do. The first is to make sure that all your clothes are clean and steamed or pressed. This will help you immediately appear to be polished and put together, which are essential for chic style.

Your accessories can also add to your chic look. Choosing gold pieces, whether they are jewelry, bags or shoes will make you look fantastic and chic. You should aim to have one gold piece that makes a statement and draws the attention of an observer to your overall look.

When pairing or choosing your base layer, go for something that is monochrome. Neutral colors are the best for helping you look as though you dressed intentionally. Then, you can add on accessories that are subtle to compliment your total look.

CALISTHENICS

Finally, do not forget to pay attention to your face. Keeping your skin clean and clear is the first step to looking chic. In addition, you cannot go wrong with well-cut hair and a bold red lip.

Now that you know how to put together the basic outfit, you need to identify your personal style so that you know how to class it up.

CHAPTER 2

Identify Your Personal Style

Each and every person is different, having a different way that they view the world and participate in it. That is why when it comes to fashion and clothing, there are so many different designers creating a wide array of interesting looks. Before you can start to develop your chic style, you need to be able to identify your existing personal style. This will help you make the right decisions to spruce up your wardrobe and your total look. So how do you try to find out what you are all about? You can follow these steps: -

Find out What Inspires You

Looking at your clothing now, you will notice that there is a consistent tone and way that you prefer to address. You need to figure out what inspires you to dress as you do. This is best done by creating a list. Write down how you like to feel when you are all dressed up, and look through a fashion magazine to identify which designers are your style icons. Y

You may also be inspired to dress like a particular celebrity, so look at the elements within their outfits that appeal the most to you. Go through a leading fashion magazine and see what people are wearing and how the outfits look on their bodies. This is the first step to understanding what makes you feel your very best.

Think about your Lifestyle

You may find that you are inspired by great evening dresses or suits that make you feel polished and sexy. The dilemma is that you cannot wear this type of clothing all day every day, as there are places where it would not be appropriate. Therefore, when working towards identifying your personal style, you need to think about your lifestyle, and what you do each day.

This way, you can ensure that the pieces of clothing you select are a reflection of what inspires you, but, they also fit into your work life, the persona you want to portray and what you have to do on a daily basis.

Consider this, you may love an evening dress because it makes you feel sexy by hugging all the right curves and giving you an amazing silhouette. Instead of wearing a sexy dress to work, you may choose to wear a pair of dark skinny jeans that hug all your curves, and top this with a white blazer which accentuates that curve of your waist. You still look and feel great, while ensuring your style and your lifestyle are at par.

Audit your Closet

Take every item of clothing that you have out of your closet, so that you are able to sort through the items that you wear. If there are items that you have not worn for at least six months, set them aside. These are the types of items that you feel do not define your personal style, even though you have not said anything out loud. Once you have sorted out your clothes, you will be left with a smaller wardrobe that reflects who you really are.

Go through these pieces and see whether any of them say 'chic.' If they do not, you will be able to purchase some wardrobe essentials which you can use to mix and match the items that you already have. When your closet is no longer cluttered, you will be amazed by how many great clothes that you actually own. A cluttered closet makes it challenging to identify your key items.

Consider your Confidence

How great do your feel when you dress you and leave your home? Are you confident and free, or do you spend a large amount of time fiddling and adjusting your clothing so that you look alright? With a world that is obsessed with smaller clothes sizes and thin figures, it is easy for anyone to feel inadequate with their personal style.

What happens, in this case, is that you sometimes end up buying clothing that is smaller than your actual size, and you attempt to squash yourself into the clothing so that you appear slimmer. This makes it a challenge for you to stand tall and feel great in what you are wearing. Being uncomfortable will not help you feel chic.

Instead of torturing yourself in this way, make sure that you always buy clothes that fit your shape, no matter what size is written on the size tag. When your clothes are well fitting, you will feel confident and look as though you are comfortable in your own style. That is the ultimate expression of Chic.

Do not Do It Alone

When you feel lost in identifying your personal style, do not give into dismay, and instead, look for someone who is professional and experienced, and can offer you help. Go into a clothing store and explain that you want to express yourself in a certain way but remain chic as well. You should be able to find an enthusiastic shop assistant who can guide you towards excellent clothing pieces that suit you.

If you are too intimidated to go into a shop, you can choose to get advice from a professional photographer who is focused on fashion. They know how to make photos fall and fit the body well so that people always look amazing. With help from the outside, you will find a way that you can accentuate your best assets while expressing yourself with class.

Be Yourself

If you have a quirky character, and like clothing that is bright and colorful with bold prints, you may be dismayed and imagine that you cannot achieve the perfect chic. To enjoy fashion, you need to embrace yourself and ever factor that affects your style. Achieving and express-

CALISTHENICS

ing chic taste is not about changing all your clothes, it is about how you choose to put yourself together.

You need to have a personal style that you can celebrate, which expresses your taste as an individual and also defines your personality. Therefore, when you are selecting clothes, use the guidelines that have been provided, and remember to stay true to yourself.

Printed in Great
Britain
by Amazon